Liz Estrada

An Adaptation of Aristophanes'

LYSISTRATA

Allen Huffstutter

Copyright © 2019 Allen Huffstutter
All rights reserved

ISBN 978-1-7369004-3-7 (Paperback)
ISBN 978-1-7369004-4-4 (Ebook)

To all of the uppity women whose courage,
inner strength, and determination has
changed the world for the better

Liz Estrada

Cast of Characters

Mistress of Ceremonies – Person who provides introduction to the play

Liz Estrada – Attractive and professional-looking 30-ish Latina

Katherine (Kat) Lonike – Very sexy late 20-ish lady

Miranda – 20-ish lady, well built with large breasts and wearing a tight running outfit

Lilly – 30-ish lady, garishly dressed

Intern – Older teenager, sloppily dressed

Female Police Officer – Dressed in police uniform but with biking shorts and a bike helmet

Reporter – Young man with a microphone

Police Officer 1 – Fat older man in full riot gear

Police Officer 2 – Fat older man in full riot gear

Stevie Munchkin – Slender effeminate man in a dark business suit

Chorus of Men – Nine men dressed in tunics. The tunics are gray and look dusty. The men's faces, beards, and hair are gray and look dusty.

Chorus of Women – Nine women dressed in tunics. The tunics are gray and look dusty. The women's faces and hair are gray and look dusty.

Mikie Pompousnous – Kat's husband, overweight man wearing a sloppy suit

Hamid – Taliban General dressed in desert combat clothing

INTRODUCTION

MISTRESS OF CEREMONIES

In 411 BC, Greek playwright Aristophanes penned *Lysistrata*. *Lysistrata* tells the story of a group of courageous women who devise a unique strategy for ending the Peloponnesian War, which had been going on for 20 years at the time the play was first produced.

Now, more than 2,400 years later, have things really changed or can we still learn from this tale? Have uppity women in the era of Trump picked up any tricks from their ancient Greek sisters? (*With a flourish*) Let us see.

ACT ONE

[Curtain rises. *Early morning. The stage is set as the interior living room of a Georgetown flat. There is a large L-shaped couch, several dining room chairs spread around a large coffee table, and a large flat-screen TV on the back wall. Along the side wall is a long narrow side table. On top of the table are a dozen champagne flutes filled with orange juice, several wine glasses, and three ice buckets with white wine bottles inside. Next to the side table is a small end table. On top of the end table is a silver coffee pot, creamer, sugar bowl, and several coffee cups. There is a door on the right side of the stage. Liz is pacing around the room. As she paces, she repeatedly opens the door, looks outside, shakes her head and resumes pacing. After a few moments, when she opens the door, Kat enters.*]

LIZ
Hey Kat, at least <u>you're</u> out and about.

KAT
Good morning Liz. Why the scowl? That "furrowed brow" look just isn't working for you.

LIZ
I know, Kat, but I'm just so pissed! Men think we are so clever and will stop at nothing to get what we want ...

KAT
Well, truth be told, aren't we?

LIZ
But when it comes to showing up this morning to plot and plan for the future of something really serious, these WOMEN lie in bed and don't show up.

KAT
They'll come. You know what it's like on a Sunday morning, rolling the old man out of bed, feeding the kids, getting everyone dressed. Everyone needs to be tended to before a women can slip out.

LIZ
But there is more important work to be done than those routine chores.

KAT
What ... ever! What's this big plan of yours? Why did you text us to meet here this morning? How much of a big deal can this be anyway?

LIZ
Very big.

KAT
And devious?

LIZ
Very devious.

KAT
Then *how* could they be late?

LIZ
Well, I guess they didn't know how big and devious. My text wasn't all that explicit. But I just had to get everyone here because, after tossing and turning for several sleepless nights, I finally figured it out.

KAT
Knowing how you like your precious sleep, this must be something big if you tossed and turned for several nights.

LIZ
So big that the very survival of the United States depends upon these women.

KAT
On these women? In that case ... God help the United States!

LIZ
It's time we women decide the affairs of State ... or soon there will be no State to save.

KAT
Then we'll take the 1% down with us by god.

LIZ

No more Georgetown elites and upper crust restaurants.

KAT

No. No more! ... But not Marcel's. We have to spare Marcel's.

LIZ

And, as for Congress and the new Administration, I can't bring myself to speak out loud of what fate should befall them ... I can only think it. Yet, if our fellow women meet here as I told them to ... the democrats, republicans, moderates, and even the libertarians ... then we, all together, can save this imperfect Union.

KAT

What reasonable or glorious thing could we women ever do? We who sit around all fancied up in our designer jogging suits, or dressed to the nines in our Lord and Taylor power suits, Louis Vuitton clutch, and Stuart Weitzman's come-fuck-me-pumps?

LIZ

Those are the very things I am counting on to save us ... spandex, perfume, Victoria Secret lingerie, and see-through nighties.

KAT

But what use can we make of these things?

LIZ

To make sure that no man in Congress ever sends another mother's precious son off to another stupid war.

KAT

Oh! Then I'll perfume up and put on my tightest running outfit.

LIZ

And make sure no Senator filibusters legislation that will provide our men with honest, living-wage work.

KAT

I'll fish out the black thong and pushup bra.

LIZ

And make sure no man in Congress lies about an opponent's position, just to score political points with his rabid, uninformed, out-of-touch-with-reality base.

KAT

I can see a <u>new</u> pair of come-fuck-me pumps in my future.

LIZ

So, don't you think these women should be here by now?

KAT

Had they known the importance of this, they would have been here long ago.

LIZ

But you see, like all good George'ntonians, they do everything too late. From Arlington, no woman is here either, nor from Silver Springs.

KAT

I'm sure the ladies from Arlington have crossed the river by now. They're always straddling *something* at this time in the morning.

LIZ

Not even the ones I expected first, those from Foggy Bottom. It's so close and even <u>they</u> are not here yet.

KAT

But one of them I know is on her way and already three sheets to the wind by now. Look, some other women are heading this way.

LIZ

And over there, others are coming.

[*Enter* Miranda *and others*]

MIRANDA

Hi Liz. Are we a little late? What's with the pout? Cat got your tongue?

LIZ
I don't think much of you for coming to this business so late.

MIRANDA
Well, I could hardly find my panties in the dark. If it's so urgent, tell us what it is. We're here.

KAT
Not yet. Let's wait a little until the ladies from Arlington and Silver Springs arrive.

LIZ
Good idea.

[*Enter* Lilly *and others*]

LIZ
Well, darling Lilly! My dearest Foggy Bottom friend! What a rosy complexion! How magnificent your figure is! Looks like you could strangle a bull!

LILLY
I think I probably could. It's the pilates and the kickboxing.

KAT
And really, what a handsome rack!

LILLY (looking down at her chest)
Courtesy of my ex-husband. He had a thing. Now all they get me is a once-over, like I'm a Guernsey off to the milking shed.

LIZ
And this other young thing ... Wherever is she from?

LILLY
Oh, she's from a prominent family. Slumming as an intern.

LIZ
By god, she represents Capitol Hill well, having so trim a ... portfolio.

KAT
Yes, by god, she does. I bet there's not a K-street position she hasn't been exposed to.

LIZ
And who is this?

LILLY
She's an honest woman from Chevy Chase.

LIZ
Oh! Honest, no doubt ... as honesty goes in Chevy Chase.

LILLY
Enough about us. Who called this meeting?

LIZ
I did.

LILLY
Then speak up; just tell us what you want of us.

LIZ
First, let's settle in. I have coffee, mimosas, and chardonnay!

[*The women all move about the set. Most of the women pick up the champagne flutes filled with mimosas and casually take seats on the couch or in the scattered chairs, which they pull in to form a semi-circle. Miranda grabs a wine glass and wine bottle. She plops down on the end of the couch with the wine bottle between her thigh and the couch arm. No one takes coffee.*]

LILLY
So, now tell us why you called us here.

LIZ
With pleasure.

MIRANDA
Your text said this is most important business.

LIZ
I'll explain. But before I do, I have one little question.

KAT
Ask away.

LIZ

Are you sad because your husbands or boyfriends are away on another tour of duty in Afghanistan? Is your life difficult because your significant other has been downsized or outsourced and can't get a decent job? Are you frustrated that politicians are more interested in managing your vagina than in managing the affairs of state?

MIRANDA

After three tours in Iraq, my Jack is off to Afghanistan. Posted as a guard for one of the Afghan generals ... to make sure the general doesn't desert.

FEMALE POLICE OFFICER

My guy has given up even looking for work. He's suffering from PTSD but is thinking of re-upping just because it's a job.

LILLY

My ex had a lot of issues ... but mainly he left me because he didn't feel like a man any more, after hearing politicians rail against the long-term unemployed as lazy, freeloading moochers.

LIZ

Underwater on mortgages ... worried about the Euro debt crisis ... exhausted from taking that second job ... no one can seem to get it up anymore except my trusted eggplant dildo. Now tell me, if I have discovered a means to fix all this, will you be with me?

LIZ ESTRADA

MIRANDA
Yes, I'm with you. I'm with you even if it means hocking my nicest dress and giving up my precious wine.

KAT
I'm in too, even if it means taking a second job at the fish market.

LILLY
To turn this mess around, I'd walk to Mount Vernon barefoot.

LIZ
Then I will tell you my plan. Women of America! ... if we intend to force the men to do all the things that need to be done to make things right, we <u>must</u> abstain ...

KAT
From what? Tell us!

LIZ
But will you do it?

MIRANDA
We will, we will, though it may kill us!

LIZ
We must refrain from having sex with our men ... Why do you turn your backs on me? Where are you going? And you ... why such a sad face ... why are you shaking your head ... why has the color drained

from your face ... why all these tears? Will you do it ... yes or no?

LILLY
 I will not. Never. Let the country rot!

MIRANDA
 Neither will I. Let the country rot!

LIZ
 So, you my pretty "take a second job at the fish market" lady? You out too?

KAT
 Anything, anything but that. Ask me to walk across a bed of red hot coals if you want, but to rob us of the sweetest thing in all the world, my dear, dear Liz, that is just too much!

LIZ
 And you?

INTERN
 Yes, I agree with the others. I too would sooner crawl across red hot embers.

LIZ
 Oh, we are a deprived sex. Poets have done well to cast our lives as tragic. We are good for nothing but love and lust. Kat, my dear friend, if *you* will join me, all might be OK. Help me, stand by me, I beg you.

KAT

'Tis a hard thing for a woman to sleep alone without a strong man in her bed. But, by the ghosts of Betty Friedan and Susan B. Anthony, the country must come first.

LIZ

Oh, my dear friend, my best friend, you are the only one here who deserves to be called a woman.

KAT

But if ... god forbid ... we do refrain from sex ... all of us ... will that really fix the country sooner?

LIZ

I am absolutely positive. If we tart up our makeup and tease our hair, put on our black nighties, employ all our charms, we will drive them mad and they'll go wild with wanting to jump in the sack. That will be when we refuse, and then they will agree to whatever we want. I am confident of that!

LILLY

Yes, just as Prince Edward abdicated the British Crown after seeing Wallis Simpson with her knickers down.

KAT

But, poor devils, suppose our men just up and leave us.

LIZ

Then we'll need to stock up on batteries for our girls' <u>second</u> *best friend*.

KAT

It's not the same. And, what if they just grab us and drag us into the bedroom?

LIZ

Grab the door.

KAT

What if they beat us?

LIZ

Then give in ... but nastily, and do it badly. There is no pleasure for them when they do it by force. Besides, we all know a thousand ways to torment them. Just keep up the tease. And don't fear ... they will soon tire of the game because there's no real satisfaction for a man unless his woman is sharing in it.

KAT

Very well. If it must be so, we are with you.

LILLY

I have no doubt that we can persuade *our* husbands, boyfriends, and lovers; but what about Congress? How can we make <u>them</u> act like adults?

LIZ

I'm confident we can persuade them as well.

LILLY
That's impossible so long as they think they're in charge.

LIZ
Ah! But I have seen to that already. The older women are taking care of that. While we have been here hatching our plan, they have snuck into the US Treasury disguised as cleaning ladies and <u>now</u> they <u>occupy</u> it.

[*Liz picks up a remote control and turns on the big screen TV. There are images of older women inside the foyer of the Treasury with the doors barricaded. The picture shifts to the outside of the Treasury where several overweight capitol police officers in full riot gear mill about.*]

LILLY
Well done! That should help.

LIZ
Then what are we waiting for? Let's bind our solidarity with a solemn oath.

LILLY
Give us the oath and we'll swear to it.

LIZ
With pleasure. Where's the officer?

[*Liz looks around for the Female Police Officer and motions for her to come to the center of the room next to the coffee table.*]

LIZ

Place your revolver on the table. And someone go get a flower to place in the barrel. We'll swear to that.

KAT

Not that, LIZ. Don't swear on a gun. Not if our oath has anything to do with peace.

LIZ

Well then. What if we sacrifice a live chicken?

KAT

This is Georgetown. Where are we going to get a live chicken?

LIZ

I have it. What if I get a large punch bowl and we fill it with Estate Bottled Oregon Pinot Noir? Can we swear to that?

MIRANDA

Ah! That's an oath that pleases me more than I can say.

LIZ

Then I'll get the punch bowl. Miranda, can you help me bring out a case of wine?

LIZ ESTRADA

[*Liz and Miranda exit stage left and return with a large bowl and a case of wine. Miranda opens the wine bottles and empties the contents into the bowl. Liz brings out a tray of wine glasses.*]

KAT
What a noble big bowl. What a delight it will be to empty it.

LIZ
Set the bowl on the ground. Now let's fill our glasses and form a sacred circle.

KAT
What a fine deep color.

LILLY
What a delicious bouquet. I can't wait for the finish.

LIZ
But first, if you don't mind, let us swear.

KAT
Then I'll be the first to swear.

LIZ
No! No woman before the others. We are all in this serious business together. So, ladies, raise your glass and repeat this solemn oath after me. No lover and no husband and no man on earth …

CHORUS
No lover and no husband and no man on earth ...

LIZ
... shall <u>have</u> me, no matter what his strength or passion or how high his mast is raised.

CHORUS
... shall <u>have</u> me, no matter what his strength or passion or how high his mast is raised.

KAT
Oh, Liz ... my knees are buckling.

LIZ
I will live in perfect chastity ...

CHORUS
I will live in perfect chastity ...

LIZ
Tarted up and dressed in my best black nightie.

CHORUS
Tarted up and dressed in my best black nightie.

LIZ
With the purpose of stirring my lover's most base and amorous longings ...

CHORUS
With the purpose of stirring my lover's most base and amorous longings ...

LIZ
But I will never willingly give in to him.

CHORUS
But I will never willingly give in to him.

LIZ
And if he forces me against my will ...

CHORUS
And if he forces me against my will ...

LIZ
I will be cold as ice and not offer one single response.

CHORUS
I will be cold as ice and not offer one single response.

LIZ
I will not aid him in any way ...

CHORUS
I will not aid him in any way ...

LIZ
... or do any of those nasty things he so likes me to do.

CHORUS
... or do any of those nasty things he so likes me to do.

LIZ

And, if I keep my oath ... there will be more wine ... much more wine.

CHORUS

And, if I keep my oath ... there will be more wine ... much more wine.

LIZ

But, if I break my oath, let my wine glass be forever filled with DC tap water!

CHORUS

But, if I break my oath, let my wine glass be forever filled with DC tap water!

LIZ

Do you all take this solemn oath?

CHORUS

We do ... yes we do!

LIZ

Then drain your glass and let's finish off the punch bowl.

[*There is sudden commotion on the big screen TV. Liz reaches for the remote and turns up the volume. Loud voices and screams can be heard.*]

LIZ ESTRADA

Off STAGE REPORTER'S VOICE from TV
It looks like the Capitol police are about to mount an assault. This is a surreal scene. I'm afraid this could get ugly. Really ugly and really fast.

LIZ
The older women are brave and I think they will be safe. But we should save the rest of the wine for another day and hurry down to the Treasury to stand with them.

MIRANDA
Don't you think the police will stop us?

INTERN
What if they arrest us and beat us with those nightsticks?

FEMALE POLICE OFFICER
They won't lay a hand on you as long as I'm with you.

LIZ
I'm not worried. They're not man enough to stop us. The Treasury doors and *our* special doors shall stay locked tight until they have satisfied all of our demands!

(*Curtain closes*)

ACT TWO

[*The United States Treasury. The façade of a Georgetown flat has been replaced by the façade of the entrance to the US Treasury. Inside the Treasury several old women can be heard milling about behind the facade. One old woman is standing behind a walker outside the imposing Treasury doors. Outside the entrance, several Capitol police officers, in full riot gear, are also milling about. Front stage right a reporter is talking into a microphone. Two police officers enter stage right carrying a large crate marked "Tear Gas." Another police officer enters carrying a tear gas gun.*]

POLICE OFFICER 1
Go easy dude. This is heavy. I don't want to throw my back out.

POLICE OFFICER 2
Never in my life did I think I'd be hauling canisters of tear gas to use on a bunch of old ladies.

REPORTER
We have breaking news that the situation here at the Treasury is escalating. We have eye witness reports

that the Capitol Police are preparing to tear-gas the elderly women who have occupied the Treasury. What's that ... more breaking news! There is apparently a group of Georgetown women descending on the Capitol police.

[*Liz and the other women enter stage right. They start tossing water balloons at the police and the crate of tear gas. The women take up a position between the entrance to the Treasury and the police. One of the police officers grabs Lilly.*]

LILLY
   Let me be. Oh! Oh!

CHORUS of OLD WOMEN (sing song *inside the Treasury*)
   We see you wretched, fat old cops.
   Be afraid 'cause we've got chops.
   Honest men don't act this way.
   One step closer and we'll make you pay.

CHORUS of POLICE OFFICERS (sing song)
   Look out, look out there's hags inside.
   Look out, look out there's more behind.

CHORUS of YOUNG WOMEN (*sing song*)
   Be afraid for we are here.
   Be afraid, we're the tip of the spear.

POLICE OFFICER 1
   Lots of big talk.

ALLEN HUFFSTUTTER

[Turns to and addresses his fellow officers.]

We can't take this crap and not do something. I think a nightstick to the side of the head would shut them up.

KAT
Get your water balloons ready in case they try to attack us.

POLICE OFFICER 2
Let's knock out a few teeth and then they won't talk so loud.

[Liz steps forward from the group of younger women.]

LIZ
Well, here's your chance big boy! Won't someone hit me? I'm standing here waiting. But be warned, come near me and I'll grab your balls like no other bitch has ever grabbed them before.

POLICE OFFICER 2
Shut up, 'cause with one swing I can end your days right here and right now.

CHORUS of YOUNG WOMEN
You lay even the tip of your finger on her …

POLICE OFFICER 2
And what? If I beat her with my bare fists, what will you do?

CHORUS of YOUNG WOMEN
 We will gnaw off your face and piss down your vacant eye holes.

POLICE OFFICER 1
 Where's Don Rickles when you need him? He'd put these shameless women in their place.

KAT
 Pick up your water balloons.

POLICE OFFICER 1
 And just what do you propose to do with those ... bitch?

KAT
 And you, Mr. Harbinger of Death. What's your plan for your smoke and fire? Are you planning to go all Buddhist monk on us and self-cremate?

POLICE OFFICER 1
 No! I'm going to roast your friends.

CHORUS of YOUNG WOMEN
 And we're going to put your fire out.

CHORUS of POLICE OFFICERS
 You'll put our fire out ... you?

CHORUS of YOUNG WOMEN
 There's nothing to it.

POLICE OFFICER 1
Why don't we just light them up like the 4th of July?

KAT
Because I'm preparing your nuptial bath.

POLICE OFFICER 1
You think you're going to bathe me, you dirty slut!

CHORUS of YOUNG WOMEN
Yes, yes, a nuptial bath ... he, he!

POLICE OFFICER 1
I've never heard such insolence.

KAT
I'm a free woman. I'll say what I want and bathe whom I choose.

POLICE OFFICER 1
Enough of this noise. I'll make you hold your tongue.

CHORUS of YOUNG WOMEN
And a jury of your peers will do what?

CHORUS of POLICE OFFICERS
Set her hair on fire and let's WACO the rest of them!

[*Young women start pelting the police officers with their water balloons*]

CHORUS of ALL the WOMEN
   Water water everywhere.

CHORUS of POLICE OFFICERS
   Enough is enough.

[*Kat throws one last balloon at Police Officer1*]

KAT
   I'm just watering you to help you bloom afresh.

POLICE OFFICER 1
   Jesus, now I'm freezing cold. (*Police officer 1 looks down at his crotch.*) And, I'm starting to wither.

CHORUS of OLD WOMEN (*sing song*)
   You've promised to torch us.
   To set us on fire.
   So, warm yourself now.
   With your own personal pyre.

[*Chorus of Old Women start to imitate a man masturbating.*]

KAT
   You're trembling. Just cold or are you nervous?

[*The women all retreat back into the Treasury and lock the door.*]

ALLEN HUFFSTUTTER

[*Stevie Munchkin enters stage right, followed by four Secret Service agents. He's talking over his shoulder to the agents.*]

STEVIE
This reminds me of the first weeks of Occupy Wall Street. The banging of tambourines, the constant railing against the MAN, the sex, the drugs. Not to mention the bad food.

Have you women no shame or sense of propriety?

CHORUS of POLICE OFFICERS (*sing song*)
You have no idea how outrageous they can be.
They've pelted us with water.
Now we look like we're drenched in pee.

STEVIE
Well, by the flowing waters of the Potomac, what do you expect? When we ourselves conspire with them in their waywardness and give them plenty of examples of perversity? Why shouldn't they start spouting off such wicked notions?
We go to the jeweler's shop and say something like: "My wife was line dancing when the post that goes in the hole in the clasp to her bracelet broke. Could you drop by the house this evening and put the post in the hole for her while I'm out at my card game?"
And now we've come to this.
What am I to do? I have to pay for the extra Humvees I've ordered for the President's personal SWAT team and I'm locked out of the Treasury!

LIZ ESTRADA

It's no use just standing here. Break out the crowbars. We'll show these women their proper place.

(*Stevie speaking directly to one of the Police Officers, who has turned to look toward the back of the stage.*) What are you waiting for ... where are you looking ... to see if the pub has opened?

Come on now. You drive your crowbar in on that side of the door, and I'll drive mine in on this side. Thrust and we'll pry this open.

[*Liz unlocks the door and comes out.*]

LIZ

No need to pry at all. I'm coming out on my own. Why all the crowbars? It isn't locks and crowbars we need so much as brains.

STEVIE

Really? You dirty slut. Where is that officer? Arrest her and cuff her hands behind her back.

LIZ

By the soul of Betty Friedan, just let him lift a hand at me and, police officer or not, you'll hear him howl.

STEVIE

You let her scare you? Grab her around the waist. You, go help him and get her cuffed.

[*Kat comes out.*]

KAT

By the will of Gloria Steinem, if you lay a hand on her I'll be of a mind to trample the shit out of you.

STEVIE

Look, now there's another one. Cuff her first. She's spouting off so much crap.

[*Miranda comes out.*]

MIRANDA

By the courage of Susan B. Anthony, if you lay a hand on either of these fine ladies you'll soon be pleading for an icepack for your nutsack after I give you one swift kick.

[*The two Police Officers run behind Stevie and cling to him for protection.*]

STEVIE

What's happening here? Where's a sniper when I need one?

(*Stevie and the Police Officers and Secret Service agents all start to back away from the three women.*)

I'll see that none of you get away with this.

LIZ

By the stubbornness of Rosa Parks, you come near us and I'll pluck out every one of the few hairs you have left on your head, one by one ... and you'll weep for each one.

STEVIE
What a cluster fuck. We must never let ourselves be bested by women. All together now, in the name of Arnold Schwarzenegger, let's form a phalanx and march against them in formation and with stiff resolve.

LIZ
One step closer and you'll find out we have four companies of fighting women inside, equipped for battle.

STEVIE
Charge! Attack their flank and cuff them.

LIZ
Oh allies, comrades, women. Sally forth and fight! Oh, vegetable venders, Oh grocery clerks, Oh hotel cleaners and bank tellers ... all.

Pelt them. Rail against them and abuse them with every curse word you know.

[*A group of the Old Women occupying the Treasury spill out the door carrying baskets of fruit and vegetables. They start throwing the produce at Stevie and the other men. The men, except for Stevie, are routed and run away.*]

Halt. Halt. Back into the Treasury. We'll forego the spoils.

STEVIE
Oh, what change in fortunes my men have suffered.

LIZ
What did you expect? Did you think you came up against a tea party of school girls? Perhaps you didn't know that women can be resolute.

STEVIE
I know they can ... when they head to the bar on Ladies Night.

[*Chorus of Men enter stage right and take their position on a three-stair riser at the back of stage right. Chorus of Women enter stage left and take their position on the other three-stair riser at the back of stage left.*]

CHORUS of MEN
Secretary Munchkin, you are wasting your breath.
(*sing song*)
Try to reason and they only roar louder.
Turn your back and you get a cold shower.
Soaked by a woman who's merely a waif.
My undershirt and undershorts are starting to chafe.

CHORUS of WOMEN
Threatening to beat us down will bring a beat-down on you.

Believe us ...
(sing song)
We would rather sit securely.
We prefer to sit demurely.
Like docile bees inside their hive.
More than happy to be alive.
So long as our honey isn't robbed.
Rousing us to a swarming mob.

CHORUS of MEN
How shall we tame these shrews?
(sing song)
This situation we can not tolerate.
These women we must interrogate.
We must find the reason behind this occurrence.
We must determine the cause of this disturbance.

STEVIE
Yes indeed.
(sing song)
I want to just know one thing first.
Why are you engaging in treason?
I insist on knowing the reason.

LIZ
To protect all the money in the Treasury from <u>you</u>. You'll have nothing to fight for without it.

STEVIE
You think it is MONEY we fight for?

LIZ

All our troubles are about money. When those in power can't cook up a war, they cook up an emergency at home. All, draining the Treasury.

Well, from now on let them cook up all of the conflicts they want. But, they'll never again fund their folly by robbing the Treasury. You can continue to elect them and give them license to spend your money ... but from now on the purse strings to the Treasury will be in OUR hands.

STEVIE

And, just what will you do with all the money?

LIZ

Now that you've asked, we'll manage the Treasury to make sure the public's money is spent wisely.

STEVIE

You'll manage the Treasury? You? You're not from Goldman Sachs.

LIZ

And why does our managing the Treasury strike you as so funny? We manage our households. We manage our household's money.

STEVIE

It's not the same thing.

LIZ

Why not?

STEVIE
Because we have to pay for our wars. There are expenses to pay for our defenses.

LIZ
To begin with, you needn't be waging war.

STEVIE
To feel safe, we need defenses and things like big fences.

LIZ
You'll be safe. You'll be secure. You needn't be frightened. We'll protect you.

STEVIE
You're not serious.

LIZ
Like it or not ... you shall be saved.

STEVIE
Pray tell me, when did it become the province of women to discuss matters of war and peace?

LIZ
I'll gladly explain.

STEVIE
Make it quick as I'm growing tired of all this talk.

LIZ

Just pay attention and keep your hands to yourself ... if you can.

Women, in times of war, have stood by patiently, putting up with whatever you men decide to do. You men never tolerate even a peep from us if we try to mention the unstatesmanlikeness of your actions and tell you in the softest of terms how much they upset us. We knew while <u>we</u> sat at home that <u>you</u> were out bungling diplomacy. If we'd ask, even with a shy, pretty smile, "How are things going in the peace talks, my dearest?" You'd answer gruffly, "What's it to you? This is man's business. Now shut up and get me a beer." And, I, of course, would shut up.

STEVIE

Well, you were doing the right thing ... shutting up.

LIZ

No matter how reckless your plans, no matter how spectacularly your policies failed, you would not tolerate even the slightest suggestion from a woman. And, as we sat quietly, we saw all of the fine young men vanish from the streets of Georgetown.

Out of desperation, women have now come together with the common cause of saving the United States from itself. So, if you'll just sit quietly and listen to us, we'll enlighten you.

STEVIE

Enlighten me? I've never heard such poppycock.

KAT
Shut up!

STEVIE
I'm to shut up and listen to you? I don't listen to hijab-wearing bitches!

LIZ
We'll fix that.

[*One of the Old Women places a chair behind Stevie and when Liz approaches him he steps backward and sits in the chair. All the women form a semicircle behind Stevie, separating him from the Chorus of Men. Liz takes the scarf off of Kat's head and wraps it around Stevie's head.*]

Do accept this gift from us. Cover your head to show your modesty. And now, not a word more sir.

KAT
And, please accept this little basket full of yarn as well. Here's some Xanax for you to suck on as you're off to market after knitting yet another scarf, as all the hejab'd women do.

From now on, <u>women</u> will see to war.

CHORUS of WOMEN (*chant*)
Come close ... reduce the distance.
It's time for resolute resistance.
We'll never weary of the dance.
As our sisters do advance.

We will follow wherever they lead.
For they are daring, yes indeed.
They have boldness in their hearts.
They are charming, they have smarts.

LIZ
(sing song)
In the spirit of sweet, sweet love.
Like the spirit of Aphrodite.
Breathing down our breasts and thighs.
An attraction both melting and mighty.
Raising passion in our men's eyes.
Raising more than idle passion.
We'll be known as the makers of peace ... and high fashion.

STEVIE
Based on what?

LIZ
Well, first of all we'll outlaw open carry.

OLD WOMAN
Yes! By Aphrodite. It's awful.

KAT
The spell of a stroll through Whole Foods is broken when some brute struts around all puffed up and packing heat.

STEVIE
They're just exercising their manly rights.

LIZ ESTRADA

MIRANDA
Well, they just look silly. Grown man carrying a 9 mm Glock while handing the cashier a coupon for the bag of Cheetos he's buying?

OLD WOMAN
I saw an obese biker with an AR 47 slung over his shoulder drive his Harley through the middle of the Saturday Market, scaring everyone to death. He stops, dismounts, takes a used Starbucks cup from his saddlebag, saunters over to one of the vendors, and fills his paper cup with kombucha.

STEVIE
But how can you protect us from all of the countries that wish to do harm to America?

LIZ
It's easy.

STEVIE
Oh please, do tell.

LIZ (*taking back the basket of yarn that had been handed to Stevie*)
If our yarn gets tangled, we take it thus, or haven't you ever bothered to watch?
(*Liz hands a balled up mass of yarn to Kat and they start to untangle it. The two women continue to hand the ball of yarn back and forth as the mess gets untangled.*) And we work it from one side and then the other, and we keep doing it until we work the tangles out between us.

And, that's exactly what we do to undo a war. We exchange ambassadors, whether you like it or not, from one side to the other, then we make the ambassadors change sides and argue the other side's positions. We continue the process until all of the tangles have been worked out.

STEVIE
Do you really think that the way you work to untangle a ball of yarn will work on the momentous affairs we men have to deal with? You fools.

LIZ
If you "statesmen" had a clue, you would approach international affairs the way we handle tangled yarn, and the world would be a better, safer place.

STEVIE
Go on.

LIZ
You start by making sure your yarn is of the highest quality. To do that you make your yarn by cleaning the wool, cleaning out all of the burrs and twigs. In your case, you clean out the government, shaking loose all of the plotters and schemers who hold key offices.

Then, you comb out the wool and put the fine wool in one basket and the wool that's full of burrs and twigs in another basket. In your case, you put the people of good disposition, be they citizens, residents, aliens, friends, allies, or absolute strangers into the commonwealth and mix them together with no fear of tangles. You put the troublemakers aside where they can no longer plot and cause problems for others.

Then you take the strands of fine wool and spin them into a fine thread. And then you gather the fine threads and weave them into a fine yarn. In your case you spin together people of good intent from all corners of the country.

As you draw the fine yarn and the citizens together into a ball that does not tangle, you have the material to sew together a sturdy coat that provides warmth and protection.

STEVIE

You want to treat the State like dirty wool that needs to be cleaned and combed? How asinine. And, what about war?

LIZ

You idiot. This has everything to do with war.

When it comes to war, we enjoy none of the honor and double the suffering.

First of all, we bear the suffering of <u>birthing</u> the sons you then send to war.

STEVIE

Not again with the childbirth guilt trip.

LIZ

Then, when we are in the prime of our lives and should be enjoying ourselves and exploiting our sexuality, you send all the men off to battle in far away lands. We end up sleeping alone.

STEVIE
Solders grow old too. Don't forget that.

KAT
Those that come back! And even if they come home old and gray, they can still find a young woman in a New York minute. But, for a woman, the window of opportunity opens and then closes quickly. No matter how dull you are you know it is true.

STEVIE
At least the old man can still get it up.

LIZ
Why have you not been struck by lightning? If you'll just drop dead we'll provide the coffin. Here's a crown of garlic for your journey to the afterlife.

[*Liz puts a crown of garlic on Stevie's head.*]

1st OLD WOMAN
Accept this can of sardines from me.

[1st *Old Woman opens tin of sardines and throws them in Stevie's lap.*]

2nd OLD WOMAN
Accept our toast for a happy journey.

[2nd *Old Woman raises a large water bottle in the air and dumps the contents on Stevie's head.*]

LIZ
Do you want something else?

(*sing song*)

Will you catch a bus or delay?
Will you run or will you stay?
Will you wait for our dead lovers' return?
And watch our hate like hot coals burn.

STEVIE (*sing song*)
What monstrous bitches to treat me like this.
You vipers coil and hiss.
I'm off to the highest court.
I'll offer myself as evidence.
I'm sure this mess will be cut short.

[*Stevie rises from the chair and slowly backs away from the women. Then Stevie runs off the stage.*]

LIZ (shouts at Stevie)
Are you accusing us of not providing a proper wake?
Are there no lessons from us you are willing to take?
We'll meet again in just a few days.
'Tween now and then you'll see the power of our ways.

[*Liz and the young women head back into the Treasury.*]

1st OLD MAN
No man can rest if he hopes to remain free.

We must prepare and stand ready for this eventuality.

CHORUS of MEN (*sing song*)
    Larger thing are in play and it's hard to tell.
    The game's afoot and things don't bode well.
    Are these women our enemy?
    Should we be afraid?
    They've locked up the Treasury.
    How will we get paid?

    Treason and treachery, trying to lecture the State.
    Suggesting we reconcile with the enemies we hate.
    Our leaders and motives they feel free to berate.
    But, not on my watch will they ever <u>dictate</u>.

[*Men pair off and start to practice slow-motion karate moves.*]

1st OLD MAN
    I must admit my rage is raw.
    I'd like to punch that old hag in the jaw.

CHORUS of WOMEN
    Even your own mother will not know you if you do.
    You'll look like hamburger when we're through.
    We'll beat your head and pummel your midsection.
    When we're through only in memory will you have an erection.

    Are we not to give the State good advice?

Will you not hear us or even think twice?
Handle affairs of State you think YOU can?
Yet doubt me because I'm not a man?
Your administration fails on every score.
All you do is get us into another ... and another
... and another war!

LIZ (*Liz steps outside the Treasury door*)
Come back inside.
(The men hurry off the stage. The women go back inside the Treasury.)

Now is the time to execute our plan.

[The facade of the Treasury is backlit so that the women behind the facade are now visible. There are cots and chairs and the women are milling about.]

1st WOMAN
I want to go home. I left a glass of excellent Merlot on the counter and I'm sure the fruit flies will have drunk it all if I can't cover it soon.

[*1st WOMAN heads for the door.*]

LIZ
Back inside!

1st WOMAN
But, I'll be right back. I just want to cover my wine and maybe stretch out for a short nap.

LIZ
We're not doing any stretching out. Remember?

1st WOMAN
But, my Merlot! Shall I let it be ruined?

LIZ
Small price for the cause.

2nd WOMAN
Oh silly me. I just remembered that I left laundry in the dryer. It will wrinkle if I don't fold it soon.

LIZ
You too? Wanting to leave over a few wrinkles?

2nd WOMAN
I'll come right back.

LIZ
You'll stay where you are.

3rd WOMAN
Oh mother of god! I think my water is about to break. I need to get home and get my feet up.

LIZ
What's this raving?

3rd WOMAN
I'm about to go into labor.

LIZ
You weren't pregnant yesterday.

3rd WOMAN
Well, I'm pregnant today and I need to go home and wait for my water-birthing midwife.

LIZ
[*Liz walks over to the 3rd Woman and taps her on what looks like her pregnant belly. There is a loud metallic clang.*]

What is this hard thing you have here?

3rd WOMAN
It is my child. It's going to be a boy.

LIZ
What BS. (*Liz raps on 3rd Woman's stomach again*) You're hiding something under there. (*Liz pulls up 3rd Woman's top and there is a large pot strapped to her belly*) And, just what's this for?

3rd WOMAN
Ah ... it's just in case I go into labor before I can get home ... you know, like the doves do ... in a pot.

LIZ
What a lame excuse. You're way too obvious. Sit here while I pass around your bouncing-baby birthing-bowl. (*Liz passes the bowl to Kat who shows it off to the other Women.*)

2nd WOMAN
I can't sleep here. I'm sure there's mice.

4th WOMAN
The wind is howling and rattling the windows. I'm sure <u>I'll</u> not be able to sleep with the constant clatter.

LIZ
Don't start acting crazy. Stop with the lame excuses. I know you miss your husbands and lovers. Don't you think they miss us as well? Isn't that the point?

The nights are just as hard for them as they are for us. But, we are women and we can bear hardship longer than the "stronger" sex. We must hold firm. And, in the end, if we stick together we'll win. My horoscope says so.

CHORUS of WOMEN
Tell us what your horoscope says.

LIZ
[*Liz picks up a newspaper and opens it.*]
"Just as the swallows that gather at Capistrano have safety in numbers from the hawk, when the miseries end, that which is over will be under."

5th WOMAN
Will we now lie on top ... I wonder?

LIZ (*continues reading from the paper.*)
"But, if the swallows begin to squabble, peck each other, and take to flight, then the people will forsake them and call their gathering a blight."

5th WOMAN
Oh, the horoscope is right.

LIZ
So, let's not bitch about the hardships we might endure. Let's pledge to suffer together — as one — for the next week. Let's fulfill the prophecy of the horoscope!

[*Curtain closes.*]

ACT THREE

[*Curtain rises. The back of the stage has broad steps rising up to what looks like a portion of the front of the Capitol building. To the left of the back of the stage is a slightly raised planter filled with shrubs and flowers. The Chorus of Men are standing on the three risers at the back of stage right. The Chorus of Women are standing on the three risers at the back of stage left. Liz enters from the door to the Capitol building.*]

CHORUS of MEN
 Let us tell you a story we heard as a child.

(*chanting*)

 There once was a fella named Jay, who refused to get married and then ran away.
 He lived in the woods getting by as he could.
 His loneliness was great and it filled him with hate.
 Since women had spurned him he found them quite nasty.
 Thus leading to his self-imposed chastity.

So ... don't be nasty and give us a kiss right here ... my dears.

CHORUS of WOMEN
One step closer and it won't take chopping onions to bring you to tears.

Now, let us tell <u>you</u> a story in answer to Jay's.

(*chanting*)

There once was a man from Nantucket, and when he saw a woman he thought ... well ... "Let's f .... it."

But, once he saw women as more than an object.
He realized his attitude had made him a reject.
He stopped only looking and started to listen.
He started to see how their intellect glistened.
This man saw the right path, which he chose to follow.
And his life became suddenly far less hollow.

LIZ
Oh, women! Come here and quickly.

[*Several women come out of the Capitol building door.*]

1st WOMAN
What is it? Tell me. Why all the fuss?

LIZ
I see a man approaching. He seems shaken and crazed. And apparently inspired by Aphrodite's power.

1st WOMAN
Whoever can he be?

LIZ
Does anyone know him?

MIRANDA
I do. That's the Secretary, my husband, Mikie.

LIZ
Then it's your duty now to roast him on the spit. Tease him and make love to him without really making love. Offer him everything. Give him nothing.

MIRANDA
I'll do it. When it comes to being a tease, I'm a pro.

LIZ
I'll stay here and tee him up for you. Now disappear and wait for my clue.

[*Mikie staggers onto the stage pushing a baby stroller. He clearly has a huge erection.*]

MIKIE
Oh how unfortunate am I. I've got the shakes like the DTs and I'm stretched like I'm on the rack.

LIZ
Who's there? Who managed to get by our guards? A man?

MIKIE
A man for sure.

LIZ
Then clear out. You're not welcome here.

MIKIE
And just who are you?

LIZ
I'm the lookout for today.

MIKIE
Then, for god's sake, call Miranda to come out for me.

LIZ
Call Miranda out? Why? And, just who are you?

MIKIE
Her husband, the Secretary of State.

LIZ
Well hello dear young man. Your name is not unknown here. In fact, you're a man of some fame. Your wife constantly calls your name. She can't pick up an apple or an orange without saying "Mikie would enjoy this so."

MIKIE
How like her.

LIZ
And if our idle chatter turns to husbands, your wife interrupts and says the rest are nothing compared to Mikie.

MIKIE
Go call her.

LIZ
Will you give me something if I do?

MIKIE
Indeed I will. Whatever I have. Whatever you want.

LIZ
Wait here. I'll go call her.

MIKIE
Hurry up! Since she departed there is no joy at home. I get so depressed. Even when I eat I can't taste anything ... I'm just so ... stiff.

MIRANDA (*off stage*)
I love him, how I love him! But, he doesn't want my love. So, what's the use of going to him.

MIKIE
My sweet Miranda. Why act like that? Come down here.

MIRANDA
[*Miranda comes out the door.*]
Come down? I certainly will not.

MIKIE
Why won't you come down when I'm calling you?

MIRANDA
Not when you call me without needing anything.

MIKIE
Not needing anything? I'm desperately in need.

MIRANDA
I'm going back in now.

MIKIE
No! Don't go. Will you at least listen to your baby?

[Mikie leans over the stroller, talking to the baby]

Call your mommy. Come on now, call your mommy!

[Mikie turns back to talking to Miranda]

What's wrong with you? Don't you have any pity for your child who for six days now hasn't been bathed or changed?

MIRANDA
Oh, I have pity. But it's his father who takes no care of him.

MIKIE
Come down ... for the child.

MIRANDA
Oh, to be a mother. I'll come down. But, just for the child.

MIKIE
She seems to look much younger. Even though everything's sideways and her anger's like a fire, all it does is fill me with desire.

[*Miranda walks down the stairs, over to the stroller, and leans in.*]

MIRANDA
Come let me kiss you ... you sweet little thing. Such a horrid father. Mommy loves you.

MIKIE
Why are you so mean, listening to those other women. I know you're suffering too. Come give Mikie a big sloppy kiss.

MIRANDA
Get your hands off of me!

MIKIE
But, you belong at home. My things, your things, everything is going to pieces.

MIRANDA
And, I should care?

MIKIE
Little do you care if your violets are dry and dying?

MIRANDA
Little do I care.

MIKIE
Our bed's been cold for such a long time now. Won't you come home with me?

MIRANDA
Not unless you negotiate a truce and end the war.

MIKIE
Well, if that's what it takes, I declare a truce!

MIRANDA
If you declare such, I will come home again ... but, not now. I've sworn to stay with the other women.

MIKIE
All right. All right. But, for now, will you at least lie down with me once more?

MIRANDA
No! Not yet. I'm not saying I don't love you.

MIKIE
You love me! Then why not lie down with me … Miranda dear!

MIRANDA
Don't be ridiculous. Not in front of the baby.

MIKIE
Oh, of course not.

[*Mikie rushes off the stage pushing the stroller. He speaks off stage.*]

MIKIE
Marty, be a pal. Take the kid home. If there's no one there, can you just sit with him until I get home with Miranda?

[*Mikie rushes back on stage.*]

There now. (*slightly out of breath*) You see there's no baby in our way. Won't you lie down now?

MIRANDA
But where, you scoundrel, just where is one to do it?

MIKIE
Behind the planter works for me.

MIRANDA
And how am I supposed to come home all prim and proper?

MIKIE
Well ... there's the fountain over there.

MIRANDA
Wait here. Let me go get a mat.

MIKIE
The ground will do.

MIRANDA
It may work for you but it isn't going to work for me. (*Miranda leaves and then returns.*)

MIRANDA
There. Now lie yourself down and I'll take off my clothes. Oh, silly me. I forgot a blanket.

MIKIE
No wait. I don't need one.

MIRANDA
That gorgeous body of yours deserves a blanket. I'll be right back.

MIKIE
First let me kiss you.

MIRANDA
Oh, very well.

[Miranda kisses Mikie on the cheek and rushes off stage.]

MIKIE
Hurry back. Oh, please hurry back.

[Miranda returns with a blanket.]

MIRANDA
Now lie down while I get undressed. Oh, silly girl. I forgot a pillow.

MIKIE
I don't need a pillow.

MIRANDA
That beautiful head of yours needs a pillow ... as does mine.

[Miranda leaves.]

MIKIE
Oh, my throbbing ...

[Miranda returns with a pillow.]

MIRANDA
Ready dear? I think I have everything we need.

MIKIE
Yes you have ... everything ... now come here my sweet. Our little friend here is certainly ready.

MIRANDA
Do you want a breath mint?

MIKIE
God, no!

MIRANDA
By god yes! You definitely need a breath mint.

[*Miranda leaves and then returns with a tin of breath mints.*]

Oh, what a ditz I am. I grabbed cinnamon and I know you like fresh mint. I'll be right back.

MIKIE
That's OK. Maybe I don't much care for cinnamon but, maybe it will remind us of our honeymoon, when you first made this same mistake.

[*Miranda leaves and returns with another tin of breath mints.*]

MIRANDA
Here, these should do.

MIKIE
I have a better idea. Now stop teasing me and come to bed.

MIRANDA
I'm coming, I'm coming. Now, dear Mikie, you will vote for peace?

MIKIE
I'll think about it.

[*Miranda runs off stage.*]

MIKIE
I'm dying here. She's killing me. She's gone and left me in torment. (*Mikie looks down and speaks to his crotch.*) She's let us both down. I must have someone to love. We, must have someone to love. Poor little guy. I want to give you what you want. What am I to do?

CHORUS of MEN
Poor miserable wretch.
Cock-blocked in your love-making readiness.
While you stand there stiff and rigid.
She talks and talks but then turns frigid.

MIKIE
I can't stand this much longer.

CHORUS of MEN
She's your undoing, that brazen hussy.

MIKIE
For love of god, I need some pussy. (*Mikie gets up and rushes off stage.*)

HAMID [*Hamid enters from stage right. Hamid clearly has an erection.*]
Where can I find the President or Secretary of State? I come with a message from Afghanistan.

STEVIE [*Stevie enters from stage left. Stevie clearly has an erection.*]
Are you a man or the tip of a spear?

HAMID
If it were that simple. I am from Afghanistan and I'm here to talk about making peace.

STEVIE
Make peace! You are clearly hiding something under your robes.

HAMID
It's really nothing.

STEVIE
Then why do you turn away? What is holding your robe out like that? Did the journey get you up?

HAMID
Not the journey.

STEVIE
I see. Well, how are things in Afghanistan these days?

HAMID
Everything is turned upside down. Our men are half crazed with lust. And our women just treat us like dust.

STEVIE
What is the reason for this?

HAMID
Afghan women, hearing the news of the Women's March, have denied all access to beds.

STEVIE
Whatever do you do?

HAMID
We walk around all doubled over moaning and groaning. The bitches have sworn that we can not so much as touch them until we have laid down our weapons and reached a peace agreement.

STEVIE
Ha, ha! So I see now. This is a worldwide conspiracy. Go and tell your elders to send back representatives with all the authority they need to make peace. I will urge our Senators to name Mikie as our representative with all the authority he needs. (Stevie and Hamid exit the stage in opposite directions.)

CHORUS of MEN
  No wild beast
  No flame of fire
  Is stronger when they cease
  Than the women we desire.

CHORUS of WOMEN
  Yet you feel compelled to make war on us.
  When you'll be better off _if_ – in us – you trust.

CHORUS of MEN
  Never will I get over my hatred of women.

CHORUS of WOMEN
Then, never will you have a vessel to come in.

CHORUS of MEN
You are right. In our haste we were quite impertinent.

CHORUS of WOMEN
You are right. In your haste you talk like jerks.

CHORUS of MEN
In the past that was one of our perks.

CHORUS of WOMEN
In the future it's patience you'll summon. And now, how about a little kiss?

CHORUS of MEN
No. Not now ... not just a little kiss.

CHORUS of WOMEN
Just one ... whether you like it or not. (*The women all rush over and give the men in the chorus a little kiss on the cheek, then return to their three-step riser.*)

CHORUS of MEN
Oh, you horrid women. How you tease us. You know, we can't live with you and we can't live without you. Come on, let's agree to not see each other as enemies. Let's seal the deal and sing a joyous song.

CHORUS of WOMEN (*sing song*)
We do not desire to speak ill of men

We just want peace and prosperity.
We just want to be heard above the din.
For in our voices comes such clarity.

[*Taliban solders enter stage right. Taliban solders all have erections. American solders enter stage left. American solders all have erections.*]

HAMID
No need for much talk. You can see the state we are in.

CHORUS of MEN
Us too. No hiding your yang or our yin.

HAMID
Does anyone know where Liz Estrada is? We've been told she and she alone will show us some compassion. Unless we make peace soon we will all need to march to the Mustang Ranch.

MIKIE
We've already thought of that. Our brothers in Nevada tell us even there the women have gone on strike. So, let's get on with it.

HAMID
We have come to make peace.

MIKIE
We are ready for peace as well. You and I can talk of peace, but we must bring in Liz Estrada, for she represents the women of the world.

LIZ ESTRADA

HAMID
Yes. You are right. We must include Liz Estrada as we bargain.

CHORUS of MEN
No need to call her. She has heard our voices and she is coming.

[Liz enters at the top of the stairs.]

HAMID
Hail, boldest and bravest of womankind. The time has come for you to show yourself as both uncompromising and conciliatory. To be bold yet humble. To use your skill and artfulness to make peace. We have ALL agreed to entrust you with ending our quarrels.

LIZ
That will be an easy task. First, you <u>all</u> need to stop trying to show who has the biggest military dick. If you do, you shall know peace.

(A burka-clad woman enters stage right wearing a sash with the word "PEACE" on it.)

Goddess of peace, take Hamid's hand and lead him as you should.

(A scantily-clad Kat enters stage left wearing a sash with the word "PROSPERITY" on it.)

Goddess of prosperity, take Mikie's hand and bring him to me.

To <u>all</u> of you powerful women, take your men's hands and bring them to me.

(*Women from Act 1 and other women dressed in burkas rush onto the stage. They match up with the men and all approach the bottom of the stairs.*)

To all of you. I am but a woman. But, I have good common sense and discriminating judgment, which I have further developed by listening to the wise teachings of my parents and by furthering my education.

My scorn for your handling of government, international relations, and the treatment of women applies equally to both sides. You celebrate before the god of testosterone, you kill and are killed, and you squander our treasure. That is my first point.

HAMID
This comeuppance is killing me.

LIZ
Now, Hamid, it is to you I speak. Have you forgotten your history before all the wars? Back to the early days of the Silk Road, when you traded with everyone from Asia to the Middle East? Back to when Amanullah Khan brought your country into the 20th century and – for a moment – women were treated as equals? Have you forgotten all of the times your women tended to your wounds and nursed you back to health? Yet, after this loving service you subjugate

your women, treat them like second class citizens, forbid them from schooling, and continue to make senseless war.

MIKIE
They do wrong. Very wrong.

HAMID
Yes, we do wrong by our women. We do! And yes, what lovely thighs they have. We should let them show them off.

LIZ
And, now to you, Mister Secretary. Have you no memory when you were fresh out of law school and struggling to get by. How can you take young men in that same situation who can no longer get jobs in this rigged economy and send them off to fight your wars?

And, now to both of you. Do you not remember standing shoulder to shoulder, Mujahedin and American Marine, fighting the Russians? Didn't you – side by side – rid Afghanistan of that scourge? Can't you remember being brothers in arms before becoming brothers at each other's throats?

MIKIE
Has there ever been a woman with more gracious dignity?

HAMID
Or a woman with a finer body?

LIZ
Enough with all the flattery. Now, tell me, how can you bear to be at war? What is stopping you from ending this hateful strife?

HAMID
We are ready if they will just give us our city.

MIKIE
What city my dear sir?

HAMID
Why, Kabul.

MIKIE
Kabul? In the name of all our fallen boys, never Kabul.

LIZ
Find something you can agree on. Now, agree!

HAMID
But, where can we stir up trouble if not Kabul?

LIZ
Ask for another place in exchange.

HAMID
How about Helmand Province, Kandahar, and Kunduz?

MIKIE
Surely not Kandahar and Kunduz?

LIZ
Don't make it too difficult. Pick two. No more, no less.

HAMID
Helmand and Kandahar.

MIKIE
Well, I'm ready to get back to mining rare-earth metals. Stick to Helmand and Kandahar and we've got a deal.

HAMID
Deal. I'm ready to start plowing my land again ... if you know what I mean.

LIZ
And, that's just what you shall do. Once the peace treaty has been signed. Now, go and make sure all of your allies are on board.

HAMID
What allies? Don't you know we are all on the same side now?

MIKIE
Let's hear it for the Taliban! Our new brothers in our ladies' arms.

LIZ
Well said! Now off to the showers and clean yourselves up before heading back to the Vets Club. There you'll find the ladies have emptied their pantries and

fixed a fine meal. After you have filled your bellies and exchanged oaths of peace and pledges to share the prosperity, each man will go home with his wife or lover.

MIKIE
Come along now men. As quick as quick can be. You heard the prize.

HAMID
You're the man! Show us the way.

LIZ (*sing song*)
All is now for the best.
Hand in hand, husband and wife.
Hand in hand, maid and lover.
It's time to party and then we'll rest.

CHORUS of WOMEN plus all of the other women on stage. (*All turn toward the front of the stage and sing song*)
We are and will be equals.
With our guidance we will prosper.
We are and will be peaceful.
Our rule will be just and proper.

CHORUS of Men and all other men on stage. (*All turn toward the front of the stage* and s*ing song.*)
You are and shall be our equal.
Our best we'll do to be peaceful.
Your soft hand of love's so adept.
Your guidance we now accept.

CHORUS of all MEN and all WOMEN [M*en and women are paired off. They join hands and raise their hands in the air. Sing song.*]
    From now on we'll all act as equals.
    Our wars will have no sequels.
    From now on we'll deal with respect.
    Peace and prosperity we'll rightly expect.

[*Curtin falls*]

www.ingramcontent.com/pod-product-compliance
Lightning Source LLC
Chambersburg PA
CBHW062148100526
44589CB00014B/1743